Forty Letters To A New Dad

Devotions For New Fathers

Steven Molin

CSS Publishing Company, Inc., Lima, Ohio

FORTY LETTERS FOR A NEW DAD

Library of Congress Cataloging-in-Publication Data

Molin, Steven, 1950-
    Forty letters to a new dad / Steven Molin.
        p. cm.
    ISBN-13: 978-0-7880-2525-9 (perfect bound : alk. paper)
    ISBN-10: 0-7880-2525-2 (perfect bound : alk. paper)
    1. Fathers—Religious life. 2. Fatherhood—Religious aspects—Christianity. I. Title.

    BV4529.M59 2008
    248.8'421—dc22

                                                                2007037903

For more information about CSS Publishing Company resources, visit our website at
www.csspub.com or email us at csr@csspub.com or call (800) 241-4056.

Cover design by Jenna Brannon and Barbara Spencer
ISBN-13: 978-0-7880-2525-9
ISBN-10: 0-7880-2525-2   PRINTED IN USA

To Marsha,
Gordie's Grandma, and
God's gift to me

Table Of Contents

Foreword

Dear Kyle,

From the moment you and Melissa announced to us last spring that we would be grandparents, it has been the focus of our lives. There is something indescribable about one's son (or daughter) preparing to have a child of their own.

So what do prospective grandparents do to pass the time as we await the grand entrance of this gift of life? Well, Mom shops, of course! In addition to her helping Melissa prepare the nursery, she has purchased a few things for the baby, but she has looked at and handled countless items. She has held up sweaters and dresses and bib overalls to imaginary babies, she has found toys for every "age" between six months and fourteen years, and she has found places in our home where our grandchild will play ... nap ... rock ... explore ... and spill milk!

But what do prospective grandpas do? Well, for me, I prayed and I wrote; it's what I do! The following pages are my thoughts for you — as a new dad — that I have jotted down over these months. They vary in their focus; some are rather spiritual, while others are practical advice, and still others, silly, random thoughts on fatherhood in the first forty days.

I realize that you don't need any advice from me; you and Melissa are going to be great parents, and while Dick and Carolyn and Mom and I stand by, ready to help in any way we can, I have full confidence in your abilities as parents. So, maybe these pages were simply written for my benefit. I don't know. But I pass them on to you, my heart bursting with pride in you ... and in the little one you are about to bring into this world. Enjoy!

Love,

Dad

👣 Day 1 👣

God Knew What You Just Found Out!

For it was you who formed my inward parts; you knit me to-gether in my mother's womb.... My frame was not hidden from you, when I was being made in secret, intricately woven in the depths of the earth. Your eyes beheld my unformed substance.
— *Psalm 139:13, 15-16a*

Dear Kyle,

Congratulations! You're a dad! And you're going to be a great one! The months of waiting are finally over, and you and Melissa now have a beautiful child. The mystery of its gender has now been revealed, and the anxiousness that every expecting parent feels has been dispelled by a healthy baby boy. Congratulations!

Isn't it amazing that you loved your son before he was ever born? It's hard to even explain to someone who hasn't shared this experience; that a love can be so real and powerful for something or someone who doesn't even yet exist. Before you ever saw his face, your heart swelled with joy and love and hopes and dreams for this little one. Here is perhaps an even more amazing fact: God saw him ... and loved him ... long before you did. Your child DID exist before his human birth ... inside of Melissa's body ... and in the eyes of God, this child was very, very real! The psalmist writes that while we are being formed in our mother's womb, God sees us, and knows us, and makes plans for us.

Psalm 139 are the words that Pastor Bagaason read to mom and me when you first came kicking and screaming into the world, and now I have the privilege of sharing them with you. Can you hear Pastor Keith, in his saying that children are special to God? This is biblical proof that Keith is right!

This child is a gift from God. While you and Melissa biologi-cally created him, God's hand was involved in the entire process, seeing what no ultrasound machine ever could. God already loves your son ... in fact, he has loved you for months! This child will want for nothing because he has parents so great as you ... and a God so great as Jesus!

So tonight, when your head hits the pillow, I encourage you to thank God for what the three of you have created: a life! And may that be your prayer every day of your life from this day on. It will certainly be the grateful prayer of four ecstatic grandparents! Welcome to the world, baby Gordon. We've been expecting you!

Love,

Dad

Lord Jesus, thank you. You have brought this child into my life and I am overflowing with love and joy. Help me to be a loving father and a model for this new life. Amen.

❪ *Day 2* ❫

What's In A Name?

And he is named Wonderful Counselor, Mighty God, Everlasting Father, Prince of Peace. — *Isaiah 9:6b*

Dear Kyle,

I love the baby's name: *Gordon.* How did you come up with it? I don't think we have any "Gordons" in our family, but I'm not sure about Melissa's. By the way, do you know what his name means? I looked it up.

> *Gordon:*   *Round hill*

While I was at it, I looked up some other names in our families.

> *Kyle:*   *Straight, narrow channel*
> *Melissa:*   *Honey bee*
> *Marsha:*   *Gracious*
> *Richard:*   *Strong ruler*
> *Kindra:*   *Clear water*
> *Alice:*   *Noble; kind*
> *Carolyn:*   *Joy*
> *Steven:*   *Crowned one*

In some cultures, names are chosen for specific reasons, as is often the case in our culture. Native Americans, for example, will name a child after an animal that is feared or respected, or name it for a characteristic that is displayed or desired. In South Dakota, we knew such people as *Martin Brokenleg* or *David Strong Bull,* remember?

In biblical times, names were given sometimes out of circumstance. Abraham and Sarah were elderly when Sarah was told she was pregnant; in fact, she laughed out loud when she was told of her pregnancy. Her son's name? *Isaac.* It means "Laugher." And Jesus had many names. In addition to those listed by Isaiah (Wonderful Counselor, Mighty God, Everlasting Father, Prince of Peace), he also is called "Jesus," which means "He will save." And of course, he has!

Gordon has a good name to live up to ... a round hill ... a solid, stable piece of ground, a place for the lamp to be set, a life where the light of Christ can be displayed. Gordon. That's a good name.

Love,

Dad

＊＊＊＊＊＊＊＊＊＊＊＊

Gracious God, may my son's name always be spoken with love and respect. And may he come to love the name of Jesus ... the one who saves his people. Amen.

Day 3

The Homecoming

As for me and my household, we will serve the Lord.
— Joshua 24:15b

Dear Kyle,

I remember the day we brought you home from the hospital. Oh, things are so different today! There were no car seats, no giant SUVs with air bags surrounding the passengers, no cell phones or OnStar in the event of an accident. Just me in the driver's seat, and your mom next to me, holding you on her lap. But did I ever drive carefully! You were the most precious cargo I had ever carried and I was extremely cautious and law-abiding along the way!

It was a beautiful autumn day when we brought you home; we walked into the house and showed you your room. Then we sat there, in the living room, wondering, "Okay, what do we do now?" Perhaps you are having that feeling today?

A home is not just where we eat and sleep and watch television. Home is where families bond, where values are taught and displayed, where we laugh, and cry, and fight, and forgive, and experience life. That's why we seldom say, "That's my house" but rather say, "That's where I live."

Within these walls, Gordon will learn how to live. He will watch you and his mom say prayers, he will learn to follow rules, he will undoubtedly learn to forgive others, and in the process, he will become a young man. In this house, he will learn the values of you and Melissa. You can't make him believe what you believe; but you can teach it and model it, and he will learn it by watching and listening to you.

Do you remember the plaque we had hanging on the wall by the front door in our first Sioux Falls house? It was given to us by Jack and Lenie Muhlenpoh — a small, crude drawing of a log cabin, snow on the roof and smoke billowing from the chimney, and these words: *As for me and my house, we shall serve the Lord.*

It was hard to miss, whenever I came and went by that door. It was a reminder that when we left our home (all four of us), we represented God. May home always be a safe place for you and your family, a place where people who know your warts and flaws love you anyway! And when you leave that home, may you remember that you are loved, and called to serve the one who thinks you are precious cargo!

Love,

Dad

Loving God, you have made us a family. Help us to make our home a sanctuary, a safe place to love you and each other. Amen.

Day 4

Wise Ones From The East!

On entering the house, they saw the child with Mary his mother; and they knelt down and paid him homage. Then, opening their treasure chests, they offered him gifts of gold, frankincense, and myrrh. — **Matthew 2:11**

Dear Kyle,

The story of the wise men coming to see the newborn king is far removed from the birth of Gordon. Gordon's not the Savior, and we're not "from the east" (though all four grandparents are very wise!). But there is something special about this remarkable relationship we anticipate having with yours and Melissa's child. For he is a gift to us, too!

It must have seemed odd to the casual observers in Bethlehem when the scholars from the Orient came with lavish gifts and words of adoration ... for a baby! Why, that child hadn't done anything great yet ... so what was the big deal? It was because Jesus was their hope for the future.

In a similar way, Gordon is our hope for the future. He not only carries on the legacy of the Golberg and Molin families, but we also know his life is filled with possibilities that we can't even see. Like the wise men, we come bearing gifts: gold, cotton, wool, hardened steel, and plastic! Why? Because he has earned them? No, but because we love him.

One year at Christmas, Mom had the bright idea that you kids would receive only three gifts from us: a "gold" gift, a "frankincense" gift, and a "myrrh" gift. In biblical times, gold was a gift of great value, so we gave you something that was quite expensive, like jewelry, or a nice clock or a lamp for your room. Myrrh was a religious gift, so symbolic of that, Mom would get you a picture book of Bible stories, or a "Nathaniel and the Grublets" tape. Since frankincense was a frivolous spice, this would be your toy, or skates,

15

or a bicycle. We only did this practice for about two years, and I can't recall if it was because Mom ran out of ideas for the "myrrh" gift ... or if she just couldn't bring herself to give her kids just three Christmas gifts!

As our grandchild grows, we will probably overdo it in the gift department. Oops! Thank you for allowing us to indulge him from time to time, and then send him home to you. I promise to respect you as his dad, but I can't promise that I won't spoil him as my grandson! Deal with it!

Love,

Dad

God of love, you place people in our paths who love us, even when they know our humanness. Thank you for grandparents. Amen.

🦶 Day 5 🦶

Sleep Is A Myth

Then Jesus told them a parable about their need to pray always and not to lose heart. He said, "In a certain city there was a judge who neither feared God nor had respect for people. In that city there was a widow who kept coming to him and saying, 'Grant me justice against my opponent.' For a while he refused; but later he said to himself, 'Though I have no fear of God and no respect for anyone, yet because this widow keeps bothering me, I will grant her justice, so that she may not wear me out by continually coming.'"
— Luke 18:1-5

Dear Kyle,

By now you have discovered that a baby's sleep schedule is not necessarily coordinated with his parents'. But further, you have likely discovered that it is virtually impossible to ignore their wet or hungry cry at 2 a.m. But what if the diaper is dry and the child has been fed? Do you allow the crying to continue? Conventional wisdom and the local pediatrician would suggest that you try to ignore it. (But I'll bet you don't outlast the baby!)

What do Gordon's cries teach us about prayer? The same thing that the persistent widow in Jesus' parable does; that if he continues long enough, you will climb out of bed and pick him up and rock him to sleep. In the same way, Jesus implies, if we knock and knock and knock on heaven's door, he will tend to our prayers. Some prayers may be answered right away, but in other cases, it may take years of pestering God for the answers.

Tonight, you will pray for Gordon, and tomorrow you will do the same. One day, he may become injured or ill, and you will wear out your knees, crying out to God for healing. You will not stop with one prayer; you will not stop praying if the circumstance is not resolved in a day or two. You will pester God! Amazingly, God invites us to do so. God does not listen to "heavenly pediatricians" as they counsel God to ignore the cries of his children, so the children will eventually be quiet. God asks that we pray without ceasing.

Why does God sometimes not answer prayers the first time? I don't know. That part is a mystery. What I do know is that God hears every prayer, and ultimately he gives us answers. But until we hear God's response to our prayers, we are invited to pester him regularly. Until justice ... or healing ... or hope ... or reconciliation occurs, we get on our knees and pray to the God who listens ... because he is God!

Love,

Dad

God, we know that many, many times in our lives, our problems are way beyond our ability to solve them. But you are only a breath away, and you love to listen to us pray. Tonight I pray for Gordon, and ask that you watch over him and keep him in your care. Amen.

🦶 Day 6 🦶

Love So Amazing!

But we were gentle among you, like a nurse [nursing mother] tenderly caring for her own children. So deeply do we care for you that we are determined to share with you not only the gospel of God but also our own selves, because you have become very dear to us.... As you know, we dealt with each one of you like a father with his children, urging and encouraging you and pleading that you lead a life worthy of God, who calls you into his own kingdom and glory. — **1 Thessalonians 2:7b-8, 11-12**

Dear Kyle,

Do you find yourselves, as parents, just staring at your baby? Waking, sleeping, eating, wiggling — it's all a joy, isn't it, studying him when he is moving or when he is still? And your heart feels as if it will burst with the love you feel, yes?

When you were born, Kyle, I never knew I had this much love inside me. I never knew I could feel this much emotion for another person. Though I loved your mom, this was different; it was an overwhelming feeling of joy and passion, and tenderness, and ... and ... and ... well, love! And every time I looked at you, I felt it more.

The verses above hold three rather dramatic word-pictures that describe how we might care for other Christians, but Paul uses the language of a parent to make his point. I don't know if I can feel so passionately about other people to whom I am not related ... but then, who knew I could feel so powerfully about you? These are the three beautiful images Paul paints:

Like a nurse [nursing mother] caring for her own children ... I don't think there is a more poignant scene of peace and tranquility than this. It is in these moments when a nursing mother and her child bond so dramatically. For the child, every need of comfort, security, attention, nurture, and dependency is met in this precious time. And for the mother, the feeling of dependency and "being needed" must be gratifying beyond measure.

We are determined to share with you not only the gospel of God but also our own selves ... Isn't this what Melissa did, and continues to do — give Gordon not only food and dry diapers and a cozy crib, but *her very self*? She allowed her body to be drained of all energy and activity in order to carry her baby. She has quit her profession, she has had her lifestyle altered, she has selflessly committed to devoting every waking moment to her child.

Like a father with his children, urging and encouraging you ... Your time will come, Kyle. As Gordon grows, your bond with him will grow stronger. He will look to you for wisdom, for guidance, and for support when life gets bumpy. You will always be his dad. Always!

Can we love others in the same way we love our children? I don't know. But I do know that our capacity to love takes a giant leap when we first see this new life that has been entrusted to us ... and this never gets old! When the second child comes, and you wonder if you have enough love within you for that one, too, ha! you'll be surprised again!

Love,

Dad

🐾🐾🐾🐾🐾🐾🐾🐾🐾🐾

Loving Lord, my heart is so full! I am learning what a dad does, but there is no question how a dad feels. Thank you for this love and joy! Amen.

Day 7

Giving Thanks

Do not worry about anything, but in everything by prayer and supplication with thanksgiving let your requests be made known to God. And the peace of God, which surpasses all understanding, will guard your hearts and minds in Christ Jesus.
— *Philippians 4:6-7*

Dear Kyle,

I don't want to say your life is perfect, but ... just about! You have a lovely wife, a beautiful son, a comfortable home, a meaningful job, and a supportive family. Yes, you have challenges — don't we all? In fact, challenges are what make it worth getting out of bed in the morning! One of your best qualities is that you are a great problem-solver — always have been! So, yes, your life is just about perfect.

I know you must be thankful to God for all of your talents and abilities. Your faith compels you to believe that everything you have, and all that you do is a gift from God. Your natural response has been akin to that adage:

Work as if everything depends on you,
Pray as if everything depends on God!

Would it surprise you to know that the apostle Paul likely wrote the above recipe for happiness from a prison dungeon in Rome? His life was far from comfortable or easy or fun ... and yet, he was happy and thankful. You know a bit of Paul's experience, because you have had setbacks and hardships and disappointment. But even in the midst of tough times, you, like Paul, have exhibited thankfulness.

Parenting can be hard work. First, there are the sleepless nights, the periods of colic, and the nagging illnesses that infants can have.

Later, it might be a physical or emotional challenge in a child, or a disobedient spirit. Still later, you may have to stand by and watch your grown children struggle with school, family, work, or relationship issues. I mentioned in the last session that you will always be Gordon's dad. Always. Even when your life might be going along smoothly, if he hurts, then you will hurt, too.

May I suggest Paul's recipe for happiness?

- Don't be anxious about anything.
- Pray about everything.
- Be thankful.
- Peace will come.

If we are only thankful when all of life is good, but not when life is difficult, then our faith is a convenient faith. But if we find reason to be thankful, even in the midst of the storms, our faith will serve us well. One thing I am thankful for — you. If your son brings you the same joy that you brought me, well ... your life will be just about perfect!

Love,

Dad

God of everything, I thank you for every gift, every challenge, and every new opportunity. I see your hand all around me, and I know that you are intimately aware of my path at every turn. Thank you, Lord, for that! Amen.

🐾 Day 8 🐾

Baptism: Blessed For The Journey

After eight days had passed, it was time to circumcise the child; and he was called Jesus, the name given by the angel before he was conceived in the womb. — **Luke 2:21**

Dear Kyle,

In every culture, there are certain milestones, certain "rites of passage" that occur during a person's lifetime. Among the Native Americans, spending a night "solo" is the entrance for a young boy into manhood. In much of the US, being sixteen grants one freedom ... and a driver's license! Jewish boys, at about the age of twelve, celebrate their *bar mitzvah*, while Jewish girls have a similar *bat mitzvah*. All of these are markers in life's journey. When Jesus was eight days old, he was given his name and went through the rite of circumcision. This always happened on the eighth day.

In the Christian church, the *entry rite* is called baptism, or, for our evangelical friends, dedication. Parents bring their infants before the gathered people of God and ask God to mark him or her as a child of God. And God does! Soon, you will bring Gordon to the font, and I will have one of the greatest moments of my life as a pastor, when I pour water over his head and say "Gordon Matthew Molin, I baptize you in the name of the Father, and the Son, and the Holy Spirit. Amen." (gives me goose bumps as I write it!)

Something remarkable happens in this moment of baptism. You turn Gordon over to God. You are still his parents, you still have to change his diapers and pay his college tuition! But now, you are his *earthly* caretaker ... Gordon belongs to God. Is this significant? Yes! Because being in God's care cannot be equaled. Loved, protected, guided, inspired, forgiven, claimed for eternity; that's what Gordon gets when he becomes a child of God. And it lasts forever.

There are other faith markers along the way: his first Bible, his first communion, and his confirmation day, but this is the beginning, his spiritual birthday.

🐾 23 🐾

When your sister was baptized, I jotted down these words, and they have always seemed to me to be an apt description:

> At the beginning of the journey
> and she doesn't even know it.
>
> In the innocence of infancy,
> She sleeps and wakes and eats and breathes
> This day and the next.
>
> Can she know what the journey holds?
> Can she possibly know about the sorrow and the joy?
> About the loneliness, the fear, the laughter, and the
>   ecstasy?
>
> Can she know what love this journey will contain?
> Or the dreams that will shatter along the way?
>
> She does not know, this little one,
> But Someone does.
> And he has marked The Promise
> upon her brow and upon her breast
> The journey would be blessed!

Over the next few years, I hope you will celebrate Gordon's baptism with him. Pray with him, light his baptismal candle, show him pictures of this day, and remind him that he is a child of God and nothing he does can ever change that fact.

Love,

Dad

Dear Lord, who can understand baptism? A little water, a promise from your Son, and a relationship that will last for eternity! Thank you for the gift you have given to Gordon. He will be my son and your son forever! Amen.

🦶 Day 9 🦶

Joy And Responsibility

Children, obey your parents in the Lord, for this is right. "Honor your father and mother" — for this is the first commandment with a promise: "so that it may be well with you and you may live long on the earth." And fathers, do not provoke your children to anger, but bring them up in the discipline and instruction of the Lord. — *Ephesians 6:1-4*

Dear Kyle,

Has the fear struck you yet? In this first week of parenthood, there is euphoria and a gladness that will not quit! But sometime soon, you may wake up at night and the feeling of responsibility may attack and overwhelm you!

You are entirely responsible for Gordon's life; you and Melissa have this awesome task of caring for another human being for the next eighteen to twenty years. "What if I mess it up? What if I make some error in judgment and it screws up the entire life of my child?" Those are the thoughts I recall having when I became a first-time parent.

No matter how many classes you had, no matter how many books you read, none of us is really prepared to do this thing about which we have no actual experience. Every one of us feels our way, doing some things by instinct, some things that we have observed our own parents do, and some things simply by trial and error.

If (when) the fear comes, you must know that both you and Melissa are people with bright minds and sound judgment and tender hearts. If you make a mistake in parenting, you ask God and your child for forgiveness, and you move on. Oh, there are things that I wish I had done differently; times when I wish I had a "do-over." But the next best thing to a "do-over" is a "do better." We can learn from the mistake and do better next time. I give a lot of the parenting credit in our family to your mom, so this isn't bragging, but we are so pleased by the way our children have grown, and become kind, productive, and faithful adults.

There is both joy and responsibility in this job of parenting. Your "report card" doesn't really come until you are nearly finished with the task. If you do everything out of love — sometimes even tough love — you will navigate the journey well. Your cheerleading section stands ready to help any time you ask. You are in our prayers daily!

Love,

Dad

Heavenly Father, you must know how this feels — watching us live our lives. There must be days when you rejoice in our decisions, and other days when your gentle hand guides us in a different direction. Give me wisdom as a dad, to raise my son in faith and love. Amen.

🦶 Day 10 🦶

Partners In Parenting

When the festival was ended and they started to return, the boy Jesus stayed behind in Jerusalem, but his parents did not know it. Assuming that he was in the group of travelers, they went a day's journey. Then they started to look for him among their relatives and friends. When they did not find him, they returned to Jerusalem to search for him.   *— Luke 2:43-46*

Dear Kyle,

Do you remember the Christmas Eve when we were gathered in the basement of Grandpa Molin's house, and Cheryl and Greg couldn't find Sarah? A full hour had passed, when one of them thought to say, "Where is Sarah?" We searched in the closets, under beds, even in the piles of wrapping paper and ribbons, but no Sarah. Finally, Greg asked my sister, "Did you bring her in from the van?" "No, didn't you?"

I loved the fact that neither one blamed the other. They considered parenting a team effort; where there is success, each gets credit; where there is failure, each takes the blame.

Even though you may have some specifically prescribed responsibilities with Gordon (it's pretty hard for you, Kyle, to do the nursing, for example), you mutually share every aspect of parenthood. There will be times when you come home from a hectic day of work and Melissa just needs to get away for a couple of hours, even if you are weary, too. Or there will be other days when your work responsibilities keep you away for many hours, and you simply can't do your part. But otherwise, you take turns changing dirty diapers, cleaning urp off the carpet, and running to the store for more congestion medicine.

There is one more thing: When Gordon gets old enough to understand "Yes" and "No," you must put up a united front with the house rules. If you and Melissa disagree, you disagree in private. But if Melissa sends him to "time out" for not eating his vegetables, you have to support her decision.

One of the regrets I have from when I was a young dad is that I didn't do much of the grunt work. I spent a lot of time with you and Kindra, took you lots of places, and changed my share of diapers. But we fell into societal roles when it came to laundry and cleaning and cooking. I see now how terribly unfair that was. When I observe you and Melissa, I already know that you have a more equalitarian relationship, and I respect you both for that. It will be good modeling for your children, too. You are a team — life partners — and your family will benefit from that cooperative spirit. Keep it up!

Love,

Dad

~~~~~~~~~~~~~~~~~~~~~~~

Dear Jesus, increase in me my sensitivity to sharing the responsibilities of being Gordon's parents. Make me mindful of Melissa's needs, and give me the strength to do even more than she asks ... because, after all, it's for this child we love. Amen.

Day 11

Flying Solo

Two are better than one, because they have a good reward for their toil. For if they fall, one will lift up the other; but woe to one who is alone and falls and does not have another to help.... A threefold cord is not quickly broken.

— Ecclesiastes 4:9-10, 12b

Dear Kyle,

I really feel bad for single parents. I watch them try to balance life and work and parenting all by themselves, and it wears me out. This doesn't even address the guilt that they so often feel (when they are at work, they feel guilty that they are not with their children; when they are with their children, they feel that they are neglecting their work).

There will be times when one of you might feel like a single parent; in fact, I hope you do. You will soon discover how valuable your partner is, for sharing both the workload of parenting and in talking through the daily joys and challenges that come along the way. Some of the greatest conversations your mom and I have had have been in bed after a long day, filling one another in on the details. So many times, I have laughed out loud when your mom told me the things you did or said. I have also been there when she confessed to me that she "lost it" with one of you children, or she didn't give you the time or attention one of you needed.

The text from Ecclesiastes says, "A threefold cord is not quickly broken." Who is this "threefold cord"? It is God. Remember that you are never alone in this venture of raising a child. God watches and protects and nudges and even moves us into action when we are overwhelmed in our lives. Through prayer, we are reminded that we are not alone. Through study and fellowship with other believers, we are shown that we are not the only parents to endure this struggle, or feel this inadequacy, or face this crisis.

You and Melissa are fortunate; you have two sets of parents who would offer — at any time — any help that you need. Gordon has an Aunt Kindy who loves him very much. You have good friends, a church family, work colleagues, and each other to keep you grounded. Don't ever think you are flying solo in this life. You are surrounded by those who love and care and stand ready to be with you. Think of us as "a fourfold cord!"

Love,

Dad

Lord Jesus, I thank you for my marriage partner! My life is made full by sharing this journey with my wife, and I can't imagine it any other way. Give her patience and strength with me, and draw us more deeply in love — with one another and with you — every day! Amen.

🦶 Day 12 🦶

Reflecting On A Miracle

For it was you who formed my inward parts; you knit me to-
gether in my mother's womb. I praise you, for I am fearfully and
wonderfully made. Wonderful are your works; that I know very
well. — *Psalm 139:13-14*

Dear Kyle,

Look at Gordon. Count his fingers: ten. Count his toes: ten. Listen to the rhythm of his heart; *boom-boom, boom-boom, boom-boom.* His eyes follow light, his lungs expand and contract, his pink body pulses with life and growing strength.

This is not a biology lesson so much as it is a creation lesson. God creates life; it is no accident. When one considers all the details that must precisely come together for life to exist, in can be no accident. Consider:

- The earth is tilted 23 degrees on its axis; 22 or 24 degrees would result in an earth covered in ice caps or in water.
- Every ear of corn has an even number of rows of kernels. Every orange has an even number of segments in it,
- Canary eggs hatch in 14 days, chicken eggs hatch in 21 days, and geese hatch in 28 days. Mallard ducks hatch in 35 days, and ostrich eggs in 42 days.
- Salmon return to the stream of their birth years later when they spawn eggs.
- There are 14 different functions that must happen in our bodies before we see an object with our eyes.[1]

What's the point of all of this? It is that God works a miracle every time a child is born. The sperm and the egg come together at just the right time to create life. All of the chromosomes match perfectly. All the dominant and recessive genes know their place.

The result is a person, with a unique body, a unique soul, and a unique personality. There is no one exactly like Gordon — nowhere and at no time in history.

I remember the night you were born, Kyle. Parents were only occasionally allowed in the delivery room, and I happened to be there. When you came out and took your first breath, I was in awe. Birth can never be routine. It is always a miracle, and when I reflect on God's activity in human reproduction, I am again amazed. You, Kyle, have a miracle in your arms. Congratulations!

Love,

Dad

God of creation, we are indeed "fearfully and wonderfully made!" Thank you for the wonder of birth, and the privilege we have in being witness to it. May we never take for granted what you have miraculously made. Amen.

---

1. Ty Saltzgiver, *Considering Christianity* (Atlanta, Georgia: Salt Resources, Inc., 1988).

🦶 Day 13 🦶

Time For A Change

Hear, O Israel: The Lord is our God, the Lord alone. You shall love the Lord your God with all your heart, and with all your soul, and with all your might. Keep these words that I am commanding you today in your heart. Recite them to your children and talk about them when you are away, when you lie down and when you rise. — Deuteronomy 6:4-7

Dear Kyle,

Ah yes, dirty diapers! This will be one of those tasks that Melissa will love to defer to you! And I would suggest that you make the most of the time when you change Gordon's diaper. How? Here's a list:

Sing to him
Tell him stories
Make him laugh
Teach him new words
Tell him that you love him
Tell him that God loves him
Tell him how much you love Melissa
Tell him how much his mom loves him
Tell Gordon that he is special
Say prayers with him
Kiss him
Hug him
Enjoy!

One of the routines we had when I changed your diaper (you were a bit older than Gordon is now), is that I stood you up and you jumped from the changing table into my arms. You used to patiently allow me to change your diaper because you knew that "thrill jump" was coming. And we'd laugh!

The verses above from Deuteronomy are known as "The Shema." The whole point that is made in those verses is that repetition is a key to learning. If we hear something often enough, we learn it, and we begin to believe it. "Hear, O Israel: The Lord is our God, the Lord alone!" If we repeat these words when we stand up, when we lie down, and when we walk along ... eventually, it sinks in as truth!

If, every time you change Gordon's diaper, you include some of those activities I listed above, it will become written on his heart forever.

I hope you have a happy, smelly time!

Love,

Dad

Gracious Lord, may the times I spend with my child become wonderful memories ... for him and for me. May they be opportunities to teach him about the most important truths of this life ... that he is special ... and that he is loved. Amen.

❦ Day 14 ❦

The Fear Of Parenting

The angel said to her, "Do not be afraid, Mary, for you have found favor with God." And Mary said, "Hear am I, the servant of the Lord; let it be with me according to your word."
— *Luke 1:30 ff*

An angel of the Lord appeared to him in a dream and said, "Joseph, son of David, do not be afraid to take Mary as your wife ..." When Joseph awoke from his sleep, he did as the angel of the Lord commanded him; he took her as his wife.
— *Matthew 1:19 ff*

Dear Kyle,

Nobody said the job of parenting would be easy. Sure, right now the greatest hardships are a lack of sleep and the cost of developing pictures! Enjoy these days, these wonderful days when you can insulate your child from most of the dangers of the world. He is safe and secure in your arms.

Growing up in this day is a scary proposition. I don't have to list for you the risks and temptations that confront the young people of our world; but we both know they are there. As your child begins seeking independence, you cannot protect him 24 hours a day. He will be vulnerable to so many things.

I am telling you what the angel Gabriel told both Mary and Joseph, "Don't be afraid!" *You surround* yourselves with quality people, *you provide* your child with boundaries, *you encourage* him to be cautious in his decisions, *you teach* him to respect himself, his family, and his name. And *you pray* that God will always be with him, wherever he goes.

Perhaps the biggest challenge in raising children is allowing them to fail at some little things, so that they know the consequences of their actions. We hate to see our children suffer, so our tendency is to rescue them ... but they never learn that way.

A young man asked an elderly gentleman: "How can I be successful?" "Make good decisions" was the reply. "But how do I make good decisions?" "Make some bad decisions."

In addition, know that you have Dick and Carolyn and mom and me, and Aunt Kindy, who hold Gordon in our thoughts and prayers constantly. Don't be afraid ... your son is in good hands.

Love,

Dad

Jesus, protect our son! Watch over him when we cannot be near. Give him a kind heart and a sharp mind to make good choices throughout his life. Amen.

🦶 Day 15 🦶

Time Out For One Another

And be kind to one another, tenderhearted, forgiving one another,
as God in Christ has forgiven you. — *Ephesians 4:32*

Dear Kyle,

Have you been out alone with Melissa in the past two weeks? My sense is that you have not. A new baby in the house has a way of commanding, not only our attention, but all of our time. It is possible to get so consumed in this little one that we forget to take care of our marriage relationship. That won't do!

My suggestion to you: date night! I know it's hard to even consider leaving Gordon with anyone yet, and you need to trust your gut on this. When the time comes, schedule a time when just the two of you can go out for dinner, or a movie, and just relax for a bit. Perhaps the entire content of your dinner conversation will be about Gordon! That's okay. It is merely evidence that he has become the focal point of your lives. Perhaps you will call Grandma a couple of times over those two hours "just to check in." That's okay, too.

Getting away on date night — not just once, but hopefully, weekly — will allow you to nurture your relationship. You are partners in this endeavor. You must make sure that you are caring for each other with the same tenderness and love that you care for Gordon. In fact, that's another "teachable moment" for him. He needs to grow up seeing that, not only do his mom and dad love each other, but that he is not the sole center of their world. I know this sounds harsh, but it is true.

To add a little excitement, plan a real date. Take turns at who is in charge making the plans. Dress up, maybe even surprise Melissa with flowers or a small gift. Put some romance back into her day. Even as much as she loves it, her day can become pretty routine and dull.

Here's my offer: a free night of Grandma and Grandpa time every other week (more often, by arrangement). If you wish, we'll come over to your home so we can put the little guy to bed in his own space. I would be certain that the Golbergs would match our offer, too. This gives you a time each week when you can get away.

Incidentally, perhaps you will one day have more than one child (hope so). Then date night becomes doubly important, and this offer becomes doubly valuable. Take care of yourself and your wife, Kyle. It's one of the best gifts you can give your young son.

Love,

Dad

Father in heaven, as I strive to be a good father, help me also to be a good husband and friend to my wife. Make me sensitive to her needs, and make me open to sharing with her my needs. Bless our marriage and bless our family. Amen.

🦶 Day 16 🦶

Each New Thing

After three days they found him in the temple, sitting among the teachers, listening to them and asking them questions. And all who heard him were amazed at his understanding and his answers. When his parents saw him they were astonished.

— *Luke 2:46-48a*

Dear Kyle,

Aren't these little ones amazing? Every day is a new adventure, and each new day brings something else that they can do. While nobody is "average" there are some developmental stages that Gordon will go through, and you will be astonished how quickly he will learn. Consider that:

- At three months, he will likely hold small objects in his hand and he will identify colors.
- At five months, he may reach out for a toy and he can recognize familiar faces (like Grampa's!).
- At seven months, he can transfer a rattle from one hand to the other.
- By eight months, he'll be able to pick up Cheerios and be able to sit up.
- At one year, maybe Gordon will be walking.
- At fifteen months, he can put small objects into a container ("Pick up your toys, Gordon!") and perhaps imitate the actions of others.[1]
- At twelve years, he'll know how to mow the lawn.
- At sixteen years, he'll forget how to mow the lawn![2]

They learn so much in such a short period that it is remarkable. You may not even see the growth because you are with him every day; but grandparents will readily see the changes, especially if we haven't seen our grandchild in a few days.

There is no *specific* timetable for all of this. Gordon will talk when he is ready to talk, and walk when he is ready to walk. Sometimes, parents get nervous because "Billy next door" can do something our child can't do, and Billy's two weeks younger! But Gordon is not Billy. Gordon is Gordon, and he will develop at his own pace.

Now there may be developmental issues that warrant a trip to the pediatrician. But chances are, each child (including yours!) will get around to accomplishing some task when they are good and ready to do so. Mom and dad will be watching and cheering and celebrating when they do (Yippee, Gordon!). Celebrate each new thing with joy!

Love,

Dad

❧❧❧❧❧❧❧❧❧❧❧

Good and gracious God, more than anything else, we want our son to be happy, healthy, and loved. May we be patient parents as our child grows, celebrating each new skill and ability when it comes. Amen.

---

1. http//:www.adam.about.com.

2. http//:www.grampysteve.com.

🦶 Day 17 🦶

Prayers For Living

He was praying in a certain place, and after he had finished, one of his disciples said to him, "Lord, teach us to pray, as John taught his disciples." He said to them, "When you pray, say:

Father, hallowed be your name.
Your kingdom come.
Give us each day our daily bread.
And forgive us our sins, for we ourselves forgive everyone indebted to us.
And do not bring us to the time of trial." — **Luke 11:1-4**

Dear Kyle,

Prayer. It's the only thing the disciples ever asked Jesus to teach them, and he taught them these words, which have stood for two millennia, and are still repeated by us. Gordon will learn this prayer — either at home or at Sunday school — but what other prayers will he come to learn?

For the longest time in your childhood, this was your bedtime prayer:

Jesus, thank you for the day. God bless Mommy, Daddy, Kyle, Kindy, Grandma, Grandpa, and everyone else in the whole wide world. Amen.

That's a good prayer.

When you were nearer kindergarten age, we would pray at mealtime:

God is great, God is good. Let us thank him for this food. Amen.

Or how about this one (sung):

O, the Lord is good to me,
And so I thank the Lord,
For giving me the things I need:
The sun and the rain and the apple seed.
The Lord is good to me.
Amen. Amen. Amen, Amen, Amen. Amen!

One of the most precious prayers I ever heard, and one I still use for illustrative purposes from time to time, you prayed at bedtime on the night of Pastor Glenn's funeral. We knelt by your bed, and this is what you prayed:

Dear Jesus,
I am glad that Glenn is with you.
But I am sad, because I will miss him.
Amen.

Prayers can be prayed in all sorts of ways; I don't think it matters to God. But this much I know for sure: God loves the sound of our voices when we are praying to him. God longs to hear Gordon pray. Teach your children well.

Love,

Dad

Gracious God, thank you for the privilege of prayer! When we tell you the stuff of our hearts, you listen and answer us. Help us to "pray without ceasing" and to teach our children to do the same. Amen.

Day 18

God, Give Me Patience ... Now!

Be patient, therefore, beloved, until the coming of the Lord. The father waits for the precious crop from the earth, being patient with it until it receives the early and the late rains. You also must be patient. — *James 5:7-8a*

Dear Kyle,

Okay, I'm the wrong guy to speak of patience! The title of this letter has been my mantra for as long as I can remember. I eat fast, I work fast, I react fast, and I wait ... fast! But that doesn't mean that I don't think patience is a virtue. It is.

Often, parents are most impatient with their own children. When little ones are exploring dandelions and four-leaf clovers in the backyard, we constantly tell them to "hurry up!" When they are visually taking in all the items on the shelves at the grocery store, we drag them by the hand because we are in a rush. When it takes our children half an hour to eat a Happy Meal at McDonald's, we remind them, "This is supposed to be a fast-food restaurant!" I am convinced that adults invented Velcro straps on shoes so that we didn't have to wait for children to tie them. Whatever happened to patience?

I have wondered if I will be a more patient grandpa than I was a father. I hope so. A friend (fellow grandpa) recently remarked that he notices the things his grandchildren do much more than he ever noticed his own children. I asked him if he could pinpoint why. "I think I was too busy to watch my children when they did things like pick up Cheerios with tiny fingers or turn the page of a book or draw a picture with a color crayon. Now that I am older ... and not so much in a hurry ... I have learned to take time to notice."

So allow me to advise you to *not* do as I did. Slow down; take time to notice the little things, and don't rush Gordon. Everything he does, even when it takes so much time, is because he is learning something new. Our hurried pace interferes with this "laboratory experience" of their young lives.

If I rush Gordon like I think I rushed you, remind me to "Slow down and explore the dandelions and the four-leaf clovers, Grampa." I'll get the message!

Love,

Dad

Patient God, I do pray for patience. I know that our adult world moves at a chaotic pace, but a child's world is wonderfully and intentionally slow. Help me to be more childlike when it comes to time. Amen.

🦶 Day 19 🦶

Speaking Of Money

He sat down opposite the treasury, and watched the crowd putting money into the treasury. Many rich people put in large sums. A poor widow came and put in two small copper coins, which are worth a penny. Then he called his disciples and said to them, "Truly I tell you, this poor widow has put in more than all those who are contributing to the treasury. For all of them have contributed out of their abundance; but she out of her poverty has put in everything she had, all she had to live on."

— *Mark 12:41-44*

Dear Kyle,

I had an interesting experience last weekend. Our church volunteered to "ring bells" for the Salvation Army in front of the local grocery store, so I took my hour. It's fun to rattle that bell and cheerily wish people a "Merry Christmas!" as they place their gifts in my red kettle. When small children put in a gift, I generally ask them if they know what their gift is used for, and if they don't know, I tell them.

Last Friday, a boy about age five was given some change from his mother as they approached the kettle. He looked at me, then at the kettle, then he began to stuff the coins into his own pocket. His mother sternly said "Chad!" He pulled his fist out of his pocket and placed the coins in the slot.

I knelt down and said, "Chad, do you know what this money is for?" He shook his head. "Some people in our town don't have very much money, and when Christmas comes, they don't have enough money to buy gifts, or to even cook a meal for the family."

Chad looked at the kettle again, and then at me. And without speaking, he reached into his other pocket and pulled out a quarter ... and placed it in the kettle. "Merry Christmas, Chad!"

Your child will want for nothing, I am sure. He probably will never know what it's like to go to bed hungry, or to not have good tennis shoes, or to not have proper school supplies. But he may meet some children who go without these things. I hope (and I expect!) that he will be like Chad. Gordon will learn to share, because he has watched his mom and dad share with others.

From a very young age, may he learn to share a portion of his "wealth." If he earns a dollar a week for an allowance, will he give a dime at church? If he sees a child without toys, will he decide to share some of the toys in his box? If he passes by a red kettle at the grocery store, will he reach deeply into his pocket and pull out his only quarter? He will ... if you do. He will!

Love,

Dad

🐾🐾🐾🐾🐾🐾🐾

Dear Jesus, you are the example of generous giving. Help me to always recognize that everything I own — even the things I earned — are really gifts from you ... for me to share. Amen.

🦶 Day 20 🦶

Your Letter Of Call

Whatever your task, put yourselves into it, as done for the Lord and not for your masters, since you know that from the Lord you will receive the inheritance as your reward; you serve the Lord Christ. — *Colossians 3:23-24*

Dear Kyle,

What odd verses with which to begin this twentieth letter! But there is a method in my madness; there is a lesson in Paul's words that come screaming down the corridors of time ... to us. The lesson is this: whatever we do in this life, we must think of it as a calling from God. Martin Luther would call it our *vocatcio*: our vocation. We tend to think our vocation is that which we get paid for, yet this is not always the case. Our *vocatcio* is that which we are called by God to do.

You are called to be a certified financial planner, and a good one, at that! You serve God by helping people get their financial houses in order, so that they prepare for a rainy day, so they position themselves to not be a burden upon their children, in retirement or death. No question, you serve God in this role.

Melissa is called at this time to be a stay-at-home mom. God has gifted and called her to do this. True, she doesn't get paid — financially — to do this, yet she knows it is her calling. In fact, she gave up one calling — that of a high school English teacher — to serve in her present calling to parent. What she does now is not any more — or any less — important than that task of teaching.

But none of us are called to just one thing. Kyle, you are also called to be a dad; to spend part of your day using your gifts in raising your young son. You are also called to play in the contemporary band at church, and to be a friend to your buddies in Salem, and to be a mentor to younger people in your office. Melissa is called to be an encouragement to other moms, to reach out to her aging grandmother, and to develop home as a secure sanctuary for you and Gordon. Perhaps one day, she will be called by God back into teaching, but for now, she has other callings.

A person may be serving God in any of these capacities. One can serve God as a garbage hauler or an accountant or a nurse or a checkout clerk. If this is what we are called to do, do it well. So this is a message to you, but also to Melissa. Sometimes, the mundane tasks we are expected to do don't seem very spiritual; sometimes, they don't seem very gratifying. But they are necessary, and God has gifted us to do them. God will reward us in the kingdom for being responsible to his call. So, Kyle and Melissa, be the best Kyle and Melissa you can be, and God will be glorified in your work!

Love,

Dad

Dear Lord, remind me that all that I do and say has an impact on someone. Let me be your servant, trusting that you have gifted me and called me to love and serve others. And may Gordon watch ... and learn ... that God has called and gifted him as well. Amen.

Day 21

Can You Ever Relax Again?

Now when Jesus heard this, he withdrew from there in a boat to a deserted place by himself. But when the crowds heard it, they followed him on foot from the towns. When he went ashore, he saw the great crowd; and he had compassion for them and cured their sick. — Matthew 14:13-14

Dear Kyle,

Do you ever feel like everyone wants a piece of you, and you don't get time to rest? I don't necessarily mean *sleep*; I mean *rest.* Sometimes, in our frenetic world, we are so caught up in the busyness of our lives, that we forget to take time out just to rest. We become overwhelmed, mentally fatigued, burned out. And still there is more to do.

As a young dad, you know exactly what this is. Your clients have expectations of you that aren't confined to an 8-4:30 schedule. Your son's awake times do not correspond to your working, eating, and sleeping schedules. Melissa's needs cannot be squeezed into your day planner, like a dental appointment; she is much too important for that! But this constant state of busyness can have a negative effect on one's energy, emotions, and attitudes.

Note Jesus' response in the text above; he "withdrew from there in a boat to a deserted place by himself." There were still hungry people in his sphere, there were still the sick, and the discouraged, and the hopeless; the gall of Jesus! He went off to a quiet place all by himself! Was it because he didn't care? On the contrary, because Jesus cared deeply, but he also knew that he had to take care of himself, physically and spiritually. So he rested.

Both you and Melissa need to do this. Melissa's days and nights can seem endless and very tiring. Your juggling of work and family has the potential to wear you out. What will you do to renew your spirit when it is dry and sagging? Something, I hope.

Years ago, there was a tiny booklet titled *Tyranny of the Urgent*, which I discovered at a very dry time in my life. The premise of the booklet is simple: the "urgent" things of our lives often crowd out the "important." Taking a nap or playing a round of golf or reading a novel might be labeled as "important" by you, but not as "urgent" as returning that client phone call or mowing that lawn or serving on that committee at church. If you asked her, Melissa would have her own list of "urgents" and "importants." It's okay to say, "No." It's okay to put off some of those things that simply must be done, and take some time for yourself, or some time with Melissa, or some play time with Gordon. If you don't do this, the weariness might just knock you flat. Take it from one who knows ... take care of yourself ... and urge Melissa to do the same.

Love,

Dad

Creator God, when you made the world and all that is in it, you did so in six days, and on the seventh day, you rested. Help me to give myself permission to rest, so that I can be renewed and refreshed to serve you and those I love. Amen.

❦ Day 22 ❦

Field Trip To The Doctor

Then one of the leaders of the synagogue named Jairus came out and, when he saw him, fell at his feet and begged him repeatedly, "My little daughter is at the point of death. Come and lay your hands on her, so that she may be made well, and live."
— *Mark 5:22-23*

Dear Kyle,

By now you may have already brought Gordon to his first well-baby checkup. I expect that all went well. Your route to the pediatrician will become a familiar one, since the average newborn visits the doctor eleven times in his/her first year. Six of those are "well-baby" visits — routine, normal, and happy. The other five, however, are related to a specific concern. Those visits usually result in a minor adjustment and the baby is just fine. Sometimes at these visits a serious condition can be uncovered.

Imagine Jairus — a wealthy, privileged religious leader who came to Jesus with a desperate concern — his daughter was ill, in fact, near death. There was no one else to turn to; so he prostrated himself before Jesus, pleading for a house call.

My prayer is that you and Melissa will never, ever have to endure this sort of desperation. But if you do, know that your prayers will be heard by Jesus. The pediatrician has been gifted to care for your child, but the rite of healing belongs to Jesus. In fact, if you were to look up the remainder of this story in Mark, you would discover that, when things got very desperate, Jesus told the father "not to fear, but to believe." Eventually, Jesus did bring about a healing.

As first-time parents, you are likely to be alarmed several times in your baby's childhood. When a fever spikes or when a rash appears or when Gordon's breathing becomes labored, what do you do? You call Carolyn or Mom. You call your pediatrician. You pray.

God understands that this child is your *life*! But pediatricians also understand this. *(Remember Dr. Blake?)* Your questions will not sound stupid. Your concern is not misplaced. Your worry is borne out of love and protection.

This is how it is when you pray to Jesus. It is like phoning a pediatrician in the middle of the night; and as there is no such thing as an unwarranted call to your doctor, so there is no such thing as a silly prayer request, or an unnecessary prayer. On the contrary, God wants every concern and every request for Gordon's life lifted up in prayer, and God will hear your prayers ... and answer them!

Love,

Dad

Healing Lord, it is my greatest fear that something should happen to our child. Please keep him healthy and safe; give us wisdom as parents to know when to seek help for him. Build up our faith, so we may know that your concern for him runs every bit as deep as our own. Amen.

🦶 Day 23 🦶

Pick Up Your Underwear!

Husbands, love your wives, just as Christ loved the church and gave himself up for her. — **Ephesians 5:25**

Dear Kyle,

Sometimes, it's the little things that matter most. This, I have learned largely by default in 34 years of marriage. But I learned it most dramatically when you were born.

You see, a mother's role is a rather thankless job. Forgive the sexist perspective here, but while the father, if he is out in the working sector, gets affirmation, positive job feedback, salary raises, and thank-you notes from satisfied customers, there is no such thing for a stay-at-home mom. Moms almost never get thank-you notes from their two-month-old infants after staying up all night when they have diarrhea. No affirmation comes when a mother sits in a clinic waiting room with seven other crying babies. And what about a salary increase for a job well done? Forget about it!

Do you know how meaningful it would be if you offered to cook dinner some night? Do you know how grateful Melissa would be if you came home and said, "Why don't you take a hot bath, while I rock the baby for a while?" How validated would your wife feel if you brought home a bouquet of daisies, or wrote a note, with a big red heart, that said, "Thank you for everything you do for our son!"? Even calling home in the middle of the day and saying, "Just thought you would like a brief adult conversation ... how's your day?" can be a day-brightener.

I wish I had known then what I know now about the tremendous stamina it takes to be a mother. That's why I have included this letter. Perhaps I am not telling you anything you don't already know; you are so much more enlightened than I was as a young father. But even you can get caught up in the rigors of your job, and perhaps neglect the little things you could do to express your appreciation and love for what Melissa is doing as a parent.

Maybe you could even ask Melissa what the three most meaningful things are that you could do tomorrow to make her day go better. She might have a list that runs a lot longer than three items, or she may not be able to think of a thing, but she will be so grateful that you sincerely thought to ask. And if all else fails, there's always chocolate!

Love,

Dad

Loving God, increase in me a sensitivity to how my wife is doing each day. Make me aware of where I can contribute to the care of our child so that Melissa feels like she has a partner in parenting. As I lift Melissa up to you, I pray that you would strengthen her for the sometimes tedious role that she carries. I love her for all that she does! Amen.

🦶 Day 24 🦶

Fun Things To Do At 3 A.M.

At that time the disciples came to Jesus and asked, "Who is the greatest in the kingdom of heaven?" He called a child, whom he put among them, and said, "Truly I tell you, unless you change and become like children, you will never enter the kingdom of heaven. Whoever becomes humble like this child is the greatest in the kingdom of heaven. Whoever welcomes one such child in my name welcomes me." — Matthew 18:1-5

Dear Kyle,

Well, the first thing that should be considered is, what are you doing up at 3 a.m. — couldn't sleep? Were you watching a late game from the west coast? Are you with a wide-awake baby? I will assume it is that last.

When the house is quiet, when your wife is asleep, and your little one is bundled in your arms as you rock, you might think you are biding your time until the little guy falls asleep. But I say, use this time to consider why Jesus loves little children so much. What is it about children that impresses Jesus so? They can't offer him anything; they can't do much but eat, sleep, poop, and cry! So why are they so special to the Lord?

Could it be their vulnerability? Their unpretentiousness? Their total dependence upon others for their existence? I think so. In our western mentality, we think reliance on self is a virtue. The less dependent we are upon someone else, the better a person we must be — strong, invincible, in need of no thing and no one.

Then along comes a child. If it weren't for its caregivers, the baby would die in a matter of hours. She needs someone to feed her, to clothe her, to change her, to guard and protect her, and even to hug her. Human touch is one of the most important things that gives a child security. Without touch, the child would likely die.

Is Jesus suggesting that we are similarly dependent upon him? Is he suggesting that if we think we are self-reliant, we would not be open to a God to love us, or a Savior to forgive us, or a cross to redeem us? The religiously proud of Jesus' day were just like that, and Jesus said that unless they humbled themselves as children, they weren't fit for heaven.

Kyle, look at your son. He is exactly the kind of person that Jesus loves the best! Pure, humble, and in need of a loving God. Oh, that we would look like Gordon when the Savior looks at us.

Love,

Dad

God, in the quietness of this night, I want you to know that my need for you is great. I can't imagine life without you! How is it that this truth is made real to me by looking into the eyes of a small child? Amen.

Day 25

The Future!

Train children in the right way, and when old, they will not stray.
— Proverbs 22:6

Dear Kyle,

What dreams do you and Melissa have for your son? Have you talked about that yet? Most of us would say that we just want our children to grow up and be happy, healthy, productive citizens. However, in all honesty, we do dream that our children will be people of great accomplishments, respected reputations, and have a comfortable lot in life. I recall hearing James Dobson say that, before they are born, we just want our children to be healthy, but that's the last time "average" is good enough! It's hard to admit it, but every parent wants their child to be a success.

The writer of Proverbs was blessed with exceptional wisdom and insight, and the words above are the evidence. Parents are not to plot their child's life out, as some may suggest the meaning of this verse to be ("train him up in the way he *should* go"), but rather, one should encourage the child to go in the way that the child is inclined; in the way he is gifted to go. Let me try to explain this.

If a person is driven by his parent to become a doctor, when he really has the personality and acumen to be an auto mechanic, that child will grow up unhappy. Even if he does grow up to be a doctor, he will likely be unfulfilled. If a child is constantly told that she must be an athlete, when she really has the gift of music, or math, or drama, her life will be one big frustration. But if the parents are wise, they will provide broad experiences for their child, so that the child can discover what it is they like, what it is they do well, and where their passions lie. Then, they will grow up and fulfill their own dreams, and not the dreams of their parents. Train up your child in the way *he* should go.

57

I know you know this: Gordon doesn't have to be a surgeon or a corporate executive or a university professor or an airline pilot ... Gordon must know that he doesn't have to be the next All-American pitcher or the next great congressman. All he has to be is the best Gordon Molin he can be: a person of character, integrity, and faith. If that is all you teach your son by the time he reaches adulthood, it will be enough. God will guide him in the rest.

Love,

Dad

Dear Lord, as Gordon grows, help Melissa and me to guide and direct him in the way he *should go. And help us to embrace* his *dreams, and not vice versa. Amen.*

🦶 Day 26 🦶

Talk To Your Dad (And Mom)!

Listen, children, to a father's instruction, and be attentive, that you may gain insight; for I give good precepts: do not forsake my teaching. When I was a son with my father, tender, and my mother's favorite, he taught me, and said to me, "Let your heart hold fast my words; keep my commandments, and live."
— *Proverbs 4:1-4*

Dear Kyle,

You know what I miss most about my dad? Just stopping by his house and talking with him. Not talking about anything in particular, just talking. When you were a little boy, we would stop by Grandma and Grandpa's on a Saturday morning, and have coffee and hot chocolate. Grandma would take you into the living room and get you set up with a book or a toy, and I would usually sit in the kitchen, chatting with my dad. As I grew older, it would just be him and me. Boy, I miss those times of being ... not a father ... but a son.

There isn't much in scripture about the relationship Jesus had with his parents. We get a glimpse of Jesus at age twelve when he is teaching the leaders in the synagogue ... and next thing you know, he is thirty years old and beginning his public ministry. Scripture is totally void of scenes of Jesus interacting with Joseph. I wonder how they got along ... what they talked about ... what advice could a simple carpenter/father give to his son, who also happened to be the Savior of the world?

While we don't see evidence of it in Jesus' life, the fact is, when sons become fathers themselves, they are still sons! The relationship between us is still a very important one ... to both of us! I don't need to give you weekly direction on how to raise your child, and you don't need to hear it! But we are still father and son, and I long to share those times with you, just talking.

Don't forget to stop by from time to time, just to chat. I relish hearing about your life, the things you're involved in, the thoughts you think, the plans you make. It fills me with pride! Once in a while, you may need someone to bounce an idea off of, and I would be delighted to be that person.

Here's the upshot of our relationship: Gordon will be watching, listening, and processing what he sees and hears. When he is grown up, and perhaps a father himself, it will be him that stops by his dad's house for conversation ... because he saw it modeled when he was just a child. I'm proud of you, Kyle!

Love,

Dad

P.S. — And the same things go for moms and daughters!

Heavenly Father, as we grow older, our relationships with our parents change ... but they're still our parents! Help Melissa and me continue to share our lives with our parents, even as we share our lives with our child. Amen.

Day 27

Telling Stories

Then Jesus said, "There was a young man who had two sons.
The younger of them said to his father...." — *Luke 15:11-12a*

Dear Kyle,

Have you ever noticed how "older people" like to tell stories? They so much enjoy reminiscing about "the good ol' days!" While it is true that they often colorfully exaggerate the details the more often they tell the story, that's okay; we enjoy listening to the things that happened long before we were born.

As the dad, you will be your child's "storyteller." Some of your stories you tell will be made-up bedtime stories about bunnies or farmers or gnomes or princes and princesses. But other stories will be of your life's events; things that your children will love to hear you tell over and over again.

Sometimes, your stories will just be frivolous, but other times they will have a purpose: a "teaching moment." Your children will learn about your growing up years, about your successes and your failures, and about the obstacles you have overcome and the lessons you have learned. They will learn about Oregon High School basketball, Melissa's surgery, her golf career, and how you met on the first day of college at Gustavus. All of this will bring great delight to your children, and will be told again and again, over future generations.

Jesus, of course, was the master storyteller. He could take an event from everyday living and turn it into an object lesson of life. Most of his stories were not factual, of course, but they both entertained his hearers and taught them valuable truths about life in the kingdom.

I expect that Mom and I will have the opportunity to tell your son some stories, too. We will tell him about the great, or silly, or crazy, or thoughtful things you did when you were young, and we will giggle and laugh! "Tell it again, Grandpa!" And I will ... with even more detail the next time!

This is how families connect with their heritage. In addition to having a future, Gordon also has a past. People whom he will never meet will have an impact on his young life because of things they said, or did, or passed down to subsequent generations. And here is an important truth: if one generation fails to repeat the stories, they're lost. When the keeper of the stories from the previous generation dies, those stories die with them, unless they have been passed on.

May your children learn that they come from proud families who have loved each other and enjoyed life. Those are stories worth telling.

Love,

Dad

God, you have made us people who value being connected, not only to our contemporaries, but also connected to those in the past, and those in the future. Help us to keep the stories alive, so that our children and their children will know that they share a proud history. Amen.

🦶 Day 28 🦶

Quiet Time

He came out and went, as was his custom, to the Mount of Olives; and the disciples followed him. When he reached the place, he said to them, "Pray that you may not come into the time of trial." Then he withdrew from them about a stone's throw, knelt down, and prayed. — *Luke 22:39-41*

Dear Kyle,

We've spent some talking about the demanding schedule Melissa has as a new mom, but we haven't discussed your schedule very much. I know that your schedule is somewhat irregular and flexible, but I also know there are times when your days are filled with meetings. You are "on stage" when you meet with clients, and you have to be on your "A" game. The driving in busy traffic, the office work, the expectations; it must be quite stressful sometimes.

Then you get home and not only are you happy to see your son, but you want to catch up with Melissa, as well. Add to this your volunteer activities, your physical fitness, and the upkeep on your house and yard. When do you have time for just you?

Look to Jesus for an example. In the hectic demands of his life, he withdrew to a quiet place to spend time in prayer. Even Jesus needed to get away from it all ... and he was God!

So, what could this mean for you? I would suggest that each day you set a few minutes aside to think and pray. You might consider getting a small Bible that you can leave in your car, or in your desk at work. Read a few verses and see how those verses might apply to your life today, and then lift up to God the important issues and the important people of your life. You need not be legalistic about this, or beat yourself up on the days you don't get to it, but taking some time regularly will encourage you and help refill your emotional tank. If you're reading these letters, then you have already established a sort of pattern. Whatever you decide to do, may it strengthen your faith and give you stamina for your day.

Love,

Dad

Lord, when life gets crazy and chaotic, and when my own schedule begins to overwhelm me, help me to turn to you for nurture, encouragement, and peace. Amen.

🦶 Day 29 🦶

Now You Know About
Unconditional Love

For by grace you have been saved through faith, and this is not of your own doing; it is the gift of God — not the result of works, so that no one may boast. — *Ephesians 2:8-9*

Dear Kyle,

Tell me, what's Gordon done lately to earn your love? Has he shoveled the driveway? Has he washed the car, yet? Has he cleaned his room or picked up his toys or emptied the dishwasher? Of course not; he's only four weeks old! And yet, he has won your hearts, and your love for him only grows with each passing day. That's how it is with unconditional love.

Conversely, what could Gordon do to make you love him less? If he hits a golf ball through the kitchen window, you might be upset, but you'll still love him. If he were to spill purple grape juice on your white carpet, stern punishment might be dealt, but he would be loved nonetheless. If, in a few years, he backs his car into yours, breaks curfew, flunks out of college, and announces that his girlfriend is pregnant — all on the same day, you may want to brain him! But he is still your son, and you will love him no matter what.

From a theological perspective, the concept of unconditional love is difficult to absorb in the finite mind. But once one becomes a parent, it all begins to make sense. We are not loved by our parents because of the things we do or don't do. We are not valued by them because we're pretty or smart or polite or athletic or humorous. We are loved ... well ... just because! Our friend used to ask his little girl, "Why do I love you so much?" and she would always respond, "Because you love me so much." Exactly!

That's how it is with God. We have not earned his grace, we could never afford to pay him for his mercy, and we can never be sinful enough to lose the relationship we have with him. The best seat in the house to come to terms with God's love for us is our love for our children. It defies reason — it just is.

So next time you look at Gordon, you are looking at a real life example of someone who is loved — unconditionally. And when he looks back at you, he sees the same thing. Joy!

Love,

Dad

Gracious God, I know that your love for me is undeserved, but I never grasped that fully until my son was born. Love so deep, so "no strings attached!" Thank you for your love, and for the privilege of loving another human in a similar way. Amen.

Day 30

The Best Month Of Your Life (So Far)!

Praise the Lord!
Praise God in his sanctuary;
praise him in his mighty firmament!
Praise him for his mighty deeds;
praise him according to his surpassing greatness!
Praise him with trumpet sound;
praise him with lute and harp!
Praise him with tambourine and dance;
praise him with strings and pipe!
Praise him with clanging cymbals;
praise him with loud crashing cymbals!
Let everything that breathes praise the Lord!
Praise the Lord!   *— Psalm 150*

Dear Kyle,

It's been thirty days since you welcomed Gordon into the world. What a month! You have rearranged your work and sleep schedules, you have curtailed your social life, you have spent hundreds (thousands?) of dollars on accommodations for this child, you have been hopelessly captured by this eight pounds of flesh and blood! It's only been a month ... and you wouldn't trade it for the world!

Isn't it amazing how quickly one's life can change? You are now into the pattern of parenthood, and perhaps it is even hard to remember what life was like before Gordon arrived. You were so footloose and fancy-free. You could come and go as you pleased, head out for pizza at midnight, if you chose. But now, there is a new sheriff in town! Now there is a reason to stay near ... and you don't mind it one bit.

Welcome to parenthood. It is a great journey that never really ends; it changes over time, but parenthood never ends. There will be challenges ahead; there will be great joy, and perhaps some hardship and sadness. But all of this is what makes the relationship between parent and child so strong and lasting. It's been the best month of your life so far, but the next best month is just around the corner. Enjoy!

In all of this, we must offer thanks and praise for the God of life. This one who guided you and Melissa in your paths, who blessed your marriage, who created intimacy, who knew Gordon before he was born, and who brought him kicking and screaming into the world. Praise the Lord!

> *Praise the Lord!*
> *Praise God in the stairway, the hallway, the rocking*
>   *chair;*
> *Praise him for his great gift of life.*
> *Praise him with crying infants;*
> *Praise him with soft music.*
> *Praise him with wooden spoons drumming pots and*
>   *pans;*
> *Praise him with laughter and loud clapping.*
> *Let all who are parents, praise the Lord!*

Love,

Dad

Gracious Lord, thank you for all your great gifts, but especially today, for parenthood. We love our son with every breath, and are grateful to you for him. Thank you for entrusting him to us. Amen.

Day 31

Rhythms Of Life

For everything there is a season, and a time for every matter under heaven:

a time to be born, and a time to die;
a time to plant, and a time to pluck up what is planted ...
a time to weep, and a time to laugh;
a time to mourn, and a time to dance ...
a time to keep silence, and a time to speak.
— *Ecclesiastes 3:1-2, 4, 7b*

Dear Kyle,

I assume that Gordon is on some sort of schedule? I mean, he must sleep certain periods of each day and eat with regularity and need his diaper changed in timely fashion. He has happy times of his day; he has fussy times of his day. While you can't set your watch by these ongoing events, you pretty much know they're going to occur every few hours or so. Yes?

There is a rhythm to being a family. Oh, I know most of the time, it seems like random chaos, especially as children get older. But if one stands back at a great distance (like, say, from a grandparent's perspective), a certain rhythm begins to become evident.

For example, once school starts for Gordon, as well as any other children who come along the way, autumn will signal a return to routine. Summertime was lax: bedtime was later, bath time may have been more infrequent, and meals happened whenever people were gathered. But when school resumes, all of this will change. Because Melissa is a teacher, you already know this ... but it will even be more pronounced with schoolchildren in the house.

Another example comes along with sports seasons. Soccer practice will happen every night at six, basketball or hockey practice will be whenever a rink or gym is available, and softball and baseball practice will be every day when it's not raining. Again, rhythm.

But in a more subtle way, rhythm happens in the lives of families. Every so often, you will be compelled to have a heart-to-heart talk with your child about their behavior and it may result in a "time out." Every so often, your heart will burst with pride at something they say or do. On a fairly regular basis, they will be hurting and will need you for comfort and encouragement. Periodically, they will go through times of questioning, challenging, testing, and wandering. While there is no set timetable for all of this to occur, if one were to carefully chart it, I think it would prove to be rhythmic.

What is the point in all of this random talk about rhythms? It is to remind you that, through it all, you and Melissa must be the constants. Your children need to know that you are there, that you are reliable, predictable, and stable. In all the ups and downs of childhood, adolescence, and young adulthood, it is a solid, consistent home that becomes the anchor of a child's life. I am so glad Gordon can count on you!

Love,

Dad

Faithful God, help me to be that solid, consistent force in my son's life. Give me wisdom and strength to be trusted by him to always guide and protect. Amen.

Day 32

Fathers And Daughters/ Mothers And Sons!

Then the mother of the sons of Zebedee came to him with her sons, and kneeling before him, she asked a favor of him. And he said to her, "What do you want?" She said to him, "Declare that these two sons of mine will sit, one at your right hand and one at your left, in your kingdom." — Matthew 20:20-21

Dear Kyle,

I can't prove it scientifically, but I hold a supposition that the relationship between a mother and son is unique, and the relationship between a father and a daughter is unique. That doesn't mean that fathers don't love their sons, or that mothers aren't absolutely giddy over their daughters. It simply means that, in my observation, dads have a special bond with their daughters, and moms with their sons.

The mother of James and John must have thought her sons walked on water! The nerve of the woman — to approach the Son of God and suggest that James and John deserved places of honor at his table! Yes, mothers are a son's greatest cheerleaders!

As for daughters, dads are more "protectors" than "cheerleaders." We tend to coddle our daughters; try to keep them insulated from all danger and harm. We let the boys roughhouse; "Boys will be boys," we say, "but this is my little girl!" You can ask Melissa if this is an accurate description of her dad.

I think the way this manifested itself in our family is that Mom cut you more slack than I did, and I let Kindra get away with more than her mom did. Whether that is true or not, you would have to have that conversation with your sister.

The point is this; both moms and dads are necessary! With each child, we perform a function, a role. Our love is equally expressed, but perhaps a bit differently toward each child. Perhaps this is all psycho-babble! All I know is, I don't want to get in between your mother and someone who is trying to hurt you. You watch, and see if this is what develops with Melissa and Gordon.

Love,

Dad

Dear Jesus, I don't know if there is a difference between moms and sons, and daughters and dads; all I know is that I love Gordon, and look forward to everything that being his dad brings. Amen.

🦶 Day 33 🦶

Gurgles And Giggles And Squeaks, Oh My!

Jesus loves the little children,
All the children of the world.
Red and yellow, black and white;
All are precious in His sight!
Jesus loves the little children of the world.[1]

Dear Kyle,

When you were only about three weeks old, we brought you to worship at a church in Rochester. Immediately, we noticed that the sanctuary was void of children! Strange, we thought. We soon found out why.

When Mom rocked you on her lap, you began to emit the quietest, most contented hum in human history! You were asleep, but you must have been dreaming of eating. "Hmmm. Hmmm. Hmmm." And then they began turning their heads! These pious, rubbernecked people made us feel like a major interruption ... and we never went back!

Some years later, when there was criticism in our church over children causing "noise" in worship (that's what they called it), I wrote the following piece and included it in my sermon the following Sunday.

Jesus, The Gospel, And Cheerio Row!
Sitting in worship, in the back few rows
The toddlers are munching on dry Cheerios
Surrounded by diaper bags, duckies, and keys
The sermon is starting "Keep the children quiet, please!"

Mother's embarrassed, Father turns red
Junior just bumped the pew with his head
Jenny went potty all over the seat
They've colored the worship book, sheet after sheet

🦶 73 🦶

When the sermon is over, when the pastor is through
I'll take the child to the nursery, that's what I'll do
I'll take her downstairs where Sundays are fun
Pick her up in an hour when worship is done
The sanctuary then will be a quieter place
To speak about tolerance, patience, and grace

Parents must do what they feel is right
Having children in worship may make them uptight
But be ye reminded of what it says in The Word
Jesus welcomed adults ... but it was children he
preferred!

Children belong in church! That's the bottom line. Yes, they might occasionally become upset and need to be walked, or fed, or entertained. But I can't think of a better place for a child to be on a Sunday morning than right there, with Mom and Dad and Jesus. Bring Gordon to worship; Jesus can't wait to meet him there.

Love,

Dad

God, you love children ... and we love you ... so we ought to love what you love. Help us to teach Gordon how to worship you ... by watching us. Amen.

---

1. "Jesus Loves The Little Children," music by George F. Root, words by C. Herbert Woolston.

Day 34

The Greatest Gift: Yourself!

So deeply do we care for you that we are determined to share with you not only the gospel of God but also our own selves, because you have become very dear to us. — 1 Thessalonians 2:8

Dear Kyle,

Parents give their children amazing things! Boxes full of toys, closets full of clothes, bicycles, books, golf clubs, skates, video games, autographed baseballs. But the one gift that is often in short supply from parents to children ... is ... time.

Recent studies show that, on average, children spend 23 hours each week with a parent and 24 hours watching television. The gap widens when those children start attending school. How much of those 23 hours are "undivided attention" is not known, but with cell phones, iPods, BlackBerrys, and ESPN, it is probably something less than 23 hours. Some parents will say, "It's *quality* time that counts, not *quantity* of time." What's wrong with both?

Not so with you! You are prepared to give your lives to your child. Melissa has essentially given up her career, and Kyle, you have already said that you won't be playing nearly as much golf in the next few years as you have in the past, and you have positioned yourself professionally to not have to work nights and weekends, a rarity in the financial planning field. All of this so that you can spend time with the child you chose to have.

Children love spending time with Mom and Dad; they thrive on the attention you give them, they can't get enough of it when they are young. (As they get older, that becomes a bit different for a while. But when they are toddlers and young children, time with Mom and Dad is the best!)

Developing consistent routines. Children look forward to doing the same thing on a regular basis. As Gordon gets a bit older, maybe he will have breakfast with you — every morning. Mom might be sleeping or off doing something else, but you and Gordon will be breakfast buddies. Or maybe it's the bedtime routine: read a story, tell a joke, drink some water, say a prayer, lights out. Every night. Or on Saturday morning you always go out for cocoa (coffee) together, and then stop somewhere to explore (hardware store, zoo, river bank, woods, high school football field, whatever). Each of these routines becomes yours, and your child will value it and remind you when it's time to go!

Unexpected times. Since you work most weekdays, what if you told your child, "I'm staying home with you today"? What a great surprise! Or when he is in first grade, you show up for lunch. Or you drive the car pool (instead of Mom) some Tuesday, and after you drop off the other kids, you go out to an afternoon movie.

Bottom line: Your kids want you for their best friend in the first several years, and you won't want to miss a minute of it!

Love,

Dad

Lord, give me wisdom to spend quality time where my heart is. May the best memories of our son's childhood always include one of us. Amen.

Day 35

One Letter From A New Dad

I thank God every time I remember you, constantly praying with joy in every one of my prayers for all of you, because of your sharing in the gospel from the first day until now. I am confident of this, that the one who began a good work among you will bring it to completion by the day of Jesus Christ.

— *Philippians 1:3-6*

Dear Kyle,

On the morning after you were born, I sat at our kitchen table and I wrote you a letter. I scribbled out some words on a page, tucked it into an envelope, and put it in your baby book. I've lost track of it since then; perhaps you even have it, I don't know. While I can't recall any longer what I wrote, what I do know is that it was a letter telling you how much I already loved you, and how I looked forward to being your dad. No matter what you would ever do or say or become — or not become — I would be a proud dad.

Well, needless to say, I am still so very proud of you. You have accomplished much, you have developed into such a fine young man, and your character is amazing. But the deal still stands: I love you, and I am proud of you, aside from everything you have done. If you ever find that letter, I hope you will read it and take the words to heart; I loved you at one day old. I love you even more today! Thank you for being a great son.

What I would invite you to do now is to write a letter to *your* son. You don't have to use the same outline I used (since I can't remember it anyway), but I encourage you to jot some notes about your thoughts and feelings about your five-week-old child. Tuck it away in a chest somewhere (but remember where you put it). Pass it on to him at sometime in the future; perhaps at a time when he doubts himself or is at a crossroads in his life.

Maybe you will leave the words in this book's Daily Journal, and share that with him some day. But try to collect your thoughts about your son right now, because they will never be so vibrant and fresh as they are in these first days.

Love,

Dad

God of all, as I write these words to my son, may they be my personal covenant with him. Help me to walk my talk and never stray from the unconditional love that I promise here. Amen.

My Daily Journal

Dear Gordon,

Love,

   Dad

My Daily Journal

Dear Gordon,

Love,

Dad

🦶 Day 36 🦶

The Ultimate Parenting Cliché: "They Grow Up So Fast!"

Rejoice, young man, while you are young, and let your heart cheer you in the days of your youth. Follow the inclination of your heart and the desire of your eyes. **—Ecclesiastes 11:9a**

Dear Kyle,

Here's a scary thought:

* In 2,100 days, your child will go off to kindergarten,
* in about 5,300, he'll be starting high school,
* in roughly 5,840 days, he'll be dating and driving,
* and 7,000 days from now, he will head off to college.

My point in mentioning these milestones is neither to scare you, nor cause you to become nostalgic before your time. It is to alert you to a truth that every parent learns (albeit, too late for some): *Our children grow up so fast!* One day, they are held securely in our arms, and seemingly the next day, they are asking for the car keys. One day, they are learning to walk, and next thing you know, they are teaching their own children to walk!

There is nothing that can slow down the growing-up process; and if there was, you wouldn't want to use it anyway. This idea of growing from total dependence to a sense of independence is the natural progression of life. When they are young they need us; when they are young adults, they presume to not need us at all. And what I have learned, both as a son and as a father, is that it eventually becomes a relationship of *interdependence*, where we need each other.

Making the best of the time our children are with us seems to be the wisest counsel. Our purpose is to do as much as we can for them, with them, and to them, so that we have no regrets when they begin pulling away, exerting their independence. I recall a young mother, whose husband was a very successful, very busy physician, sitting across from me, saying, "When our children are grown up, if my husband ever says, 'I wish I would have spent more time with my children,' I will slap him silly!" So many parents look back to those hectic, busy days, and they live with so much regret.

An investment of your time and energy now will pay great dividends when your kids are grown up. Just ask your mom and me! We may not have been perfect parents, but we wouldn't trade a moment of it!

Love,

Dad

✦✦✦✦✦✦✦✦✦✦✦✦

Dear heavenly Father, your Son's earthly life was only 33 years. I am sure that Joseph and Mary were astonished how quickly Jesus grew up. Help me to treasure every day of Gordon's childhood. In times of tension, give me patience; in times of joy, let me shower it upon him; and in times of chaos and craziness, let me live in such a way that Gordon knows he is among my highest priorities. Amen.

The Worst Day Of Parenting Is Better Than ...

But Abram said, "O Lord God, what will you give me, for I continue childless, and the heir of my house is Eliezer of Damascus?"
— Genesis 15:2

Dear Kyle,

No children. That was the curse for Abraham and Sarah. That is seemingly a curse for some couples in our society today; perhaps you even know some. They have tried and tried, and yet they are unable to conceive and bear children. Each time they see a pregnant couple, their hearts break. Each time they see small children, at the mall, at church, or at the entrance of schools, they weep a thousand tears.

Of course, the story for Abraham and Sarah turned out favorably; Sarah gave birth to a son and named him Isaac. But for many couples, their hopes for a child of their own are never realized.

There will be frustrating days for you. Oh, they may not come this week, or the next, or even this year. But every parent has days of frustration and even anger at their child. When those days arrive, remember the Abrahams and the Sarahs of this age; those childless parents who would trade places with you in a heartbeat. God has blessed you richly in the birth of your son, and you must never take him for granted. Your life changed forever the day Gordon was born, and even on the days with spilled milk, a "D" in algebra, or a ding in the new car door, he is — and will always be — God's blessing to you! Rejoice!

There is something else you can do. You can carry with you a sensitivity toward those without children. Just being aware that they may be in your midst will cause you to be gracious and caring toward them. They may even want to share their pain, just to have someone listen. Do your best to be an encouragement to them, and then go home and hug the gift that God has given to you.

Love,

Dad

~~~~~~~~~~~~~~~~~~~~~~~~

God, again today I thank you for the gift of a son. May I always be grateful for his presence in our lives, and the privilege of being his dad. Amen.

❦ Day 38 ❦

What You Promised

Love is patient, love is kind; love is not envious or boastful or arrogant ... It bears all things, believes all things, hopes all things, endures all things. — *1 Corinthians 13:4, 7*

Dear Kyle,

I can't remember if you had these scripture verses read at your wedding ceremony; many couples do. It is Paul's summation of what love would look like for the Christian. When we read it at a wedding, it sounds nice; it sounds like something a husband and a wife would aspire to exhibit toward one another. It doesn't always work out that way, but on one's wedding day, it sounds like a good plan.

When you knew you were going to have a child, you made plans to love it. Gender didn't matter, shape and size didn't matter, condition of the baby didn't matter; you would love it, no matter what. In Paul's own words, this is what you promised to Gordon.

You promised that your love would be patient. Children can try the patience of a parent. I don't think they try to do so, but a child's sense of time is different than an adult's. A child is doing things for a first or second time that we have done countless times over our years. A child is an emerging personality. While it is tempting to become impatient with them, when we promise to love our children, it means that we will try to exercise patience.

You promised that your love would be kind. This means that you are compelled to be nice to your son, not mean-spirited, or rude, or ill-tempered. It sounds so incomprehensible, I know that you might treat your child with anything but kindness. Yet, when life gets hard (and it may not even be about something Gordon has done or said), you might find yourself feeling less than kind.

You said that your love would not be arrogant. I think that means that when you have made a mistake, when you have done or said something to your son that you regret, you admit it. You might even ask for forgiveness. Recognize those words? I've done that with you. I'm not elevating myself for that, I am simply saying that parents need to be most real with those they love the most ... like their children!

What is the payoff in all of this love? That even through the bumps and turns, love hopes and believes and bears and endures it all. Love: It's a beautiful thing!

Love,

Dad

Loving God, help me keep my promises to Gordon; to love him no matter what! And help me to be a role model for him to learn to love others. Amen.

🐾 Day 39 🐾

Is This What You Thought It Would Be?

And not only that, but we also boast in our sufferings, knowing that suffering produces endurance, and endurance produces character, and character produces hope, and hope does not disappoint us. — **Romans 5:3-5a**

Dear Kyle,

It's been nearly six weeks. Whew! What a whirlwind of joy, sleeplessness, contentedness, bewilderment, concern, peace, thanksgiving, pride, and a steep learning curve. And this is just the first six weeks!

Because of your passion for athletics, you might resonate with the words of Romans above. This progression from trials ... to perseverance ... to character ... to hope. Sports are like that. We learn so much about life when we are part of a team that overcomes adversity and achieves something.

Even more so, the same can be said about parenting. I think raising two children taught me more about my faith, and more about living life one day at a time, than anything else in my 55 years. Life does not always progress in a straight line. There are setbacks, and starts and stops, and exciting progress and disappointing detours. But in parenting, as in sports, as in living, one gets the feeling that we learn and grow along the way. Adversity is a better teacher than success!

I can't wait to watch you as a dad. I know you are going to be wise, and fun, and both firm and tender, and a wonderful model for your son. When the tough times come, you will approach them as you approach most things; with calm and thoughtful determination. The journey will not be easy, but it will be worth it!

I wonder if Paul really "exulted in tribulation"? Nobody loves hardship, but I believe that each life contains some, and while we cannot avoid it, we can learn to address it, find a way through it, and come out stronger on the other side.

Kyle, don't underestimate the place of faith in all of this. Because there will be days when things will look grim, and when you can't see the hope on the other side. Remember Paul's words: that first comes the tribulation, then the perseverance, then the character, and finally, the hope.

Looking back over the past 39 days, is it what you expected? I'll bet it's better! I learned that parenting is the most gratifying role I ever played in my life! I think you will discover the same. Thanks for being a great dad.

Love,

Dad

~~~~~~~~~~~~~~~~~~~~

Dear Jesus, it is better! Being a father to Gordon is both amazing and intimidating at the same time. Help Melissa and me to do our best, enjoying each day, and teaching our son to do the same. I love you, Jesus. Amen.

🦶 Day 40 🦶

Enjoying The Job That Never Ends

Beloved, I do not consider that I have made it my own; but this one thing I do: forgetting what lies behind and straining forward to what lies ahead, I press on toward the goal for the prize of the heavenly call of God in Christ Jesus. — *Philippians 3:13-14*

Dear Kyle,

I started working on this project about three months before the birth of your child. I mentioned in the foreword that I was convinced that you would be a great dad and would not need any advice or direction from me. I still believe that! I also mentioned that this might be an exercise that would benefit me more than you. That's still true, as well.

Here is what I learned in this process: Parenting is one of those things that we never get totally right, and it's a job that we keep doing until we die. Why? For the parent? No, for the child. I am 55 years old, you are now 30, and yet I still want to be a good parent to you, taking all of the advice and admonitions in these past pages upon myself because I want you to have a future.

My days as a son are over, since both of my parents are gone. But I am still your dad, and I want to be there for you in any way I can, still offering you my support, love, encouragement, and prayers on your behalf. It is not a role I have perfected! I am still trying to get it right. Maybe that's the lesson to be learned by you (if you are still reading this thing forty days later), that being a dad is a marathon, it's not a sprint.

The stupid things I did as a father when you were only two months old ... those happened 29 years ago. They are in the past! I can let them go. Now, the goal I strain for is seeing you be a good dad to your son. It is tremendously fulfilling to watch you and Melissa take the things you learned as children, and now apply them as parents.

It would be dishonest if I didn't clarify Paul's words above. They were not written to describe Paul achieving some human, worldly goal. His goal was eternal life in Jesus Christ. That's why we can be so secure in our lives, because our eternity is not dependent on something we did 29 years ago; it rests upon what Jesus did more than 2,000 years ago. The only thing that remains for us is the goal — the crown — life with the ultimate Father! If I have taught you this, it's all you need to know about a father's love. I love you. You love Gordon. And God loves us all!

Love,

Dad

Father in heaven, thank you for families! They mold us into what we are ... and what we become. Thank you for my parents and sister; thank you for Melissa's family for becoming "family" to me! Thank you for my wife, my son, my faith, my eternity — all gifts from you. Amen.

Postscript

Dear Kyle,

I met Gordon yesterday! What inexpressible joy, when you walked down the hospital corridor and announced to all of us "Well ... it's a boy!" My heart burst for you and Melissa!

When Melissa introduced us to Gordon, my heart cried out again. When I touched his toe ... when I heard his quiet, raspy cry, when I watched your mom hold him, when I saw you reach down when no one else was looking and kiss his head. Oh, it was such a powerful feeling in that room!

Most of this book has been about being a father, but this page is about being a grandfather. I love your son with a full heart — with an overflowing heart! I saw it in Mom, and Carolyn and Dick, too — this pride in seeing our lives extended through Melissa and you, and now to Gordon. He has carved out a place in our hearts that is so precious, it almost hurts! I can't explain how that feels, but it is so real.

We will be Gordon's greatest fans. I commit to him that I will pray for him every day, and he will see and hear and feel our love in a million different ways. This grandparent thing, it's all new to me. It feels different than when you were born — more humbling, and quietly joyous. I can't wait to see how it all works out ... but I am ready.

Love,

Grampa

CPSIA information can be obtained
at www.ICGtesting.com
Printed in the USA
LVHW030718201218
600904LV00001B/22/P